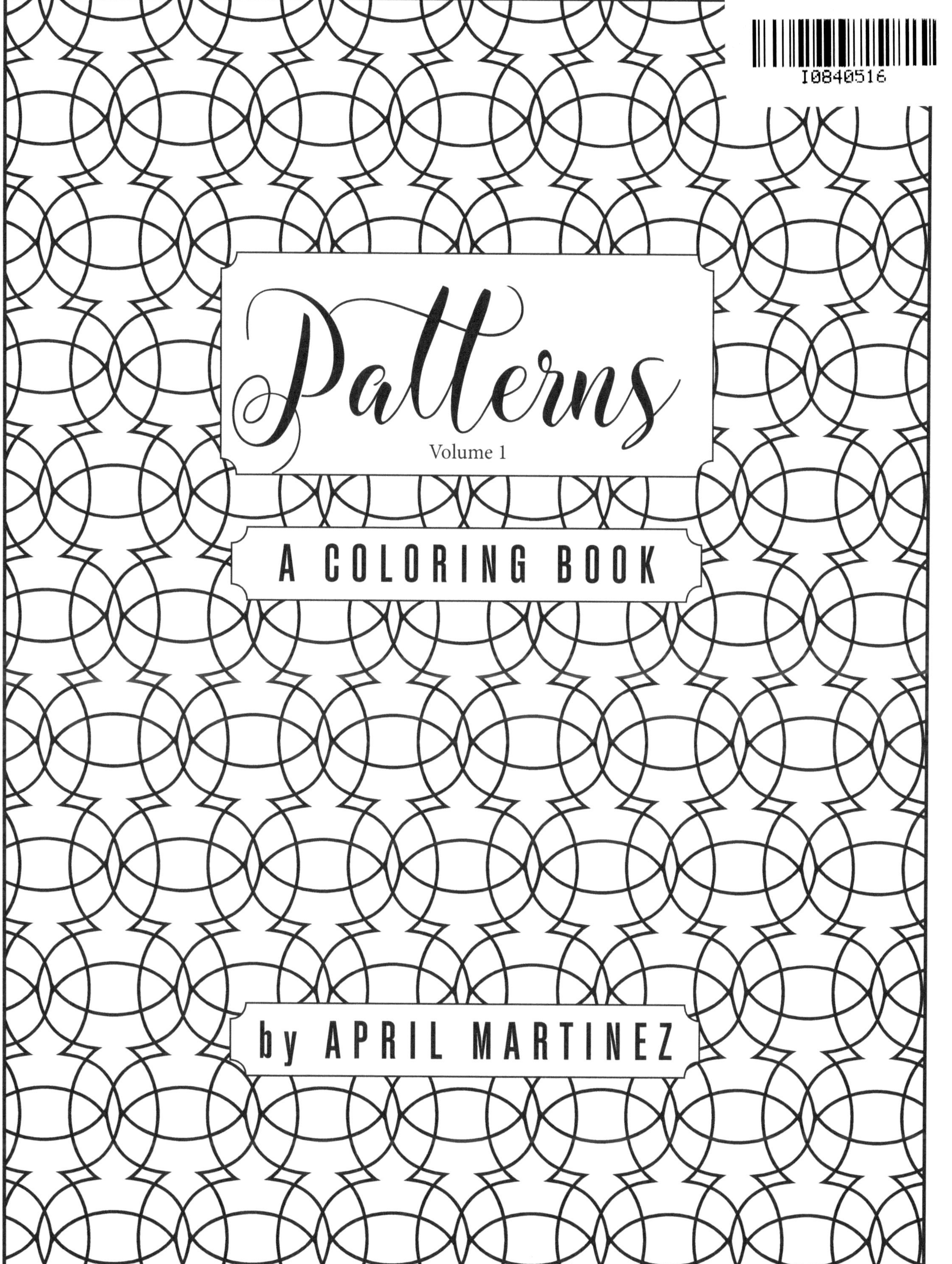

Patterns
Volume 1
A COLORING BOOK
by APRIL MARTINEZ

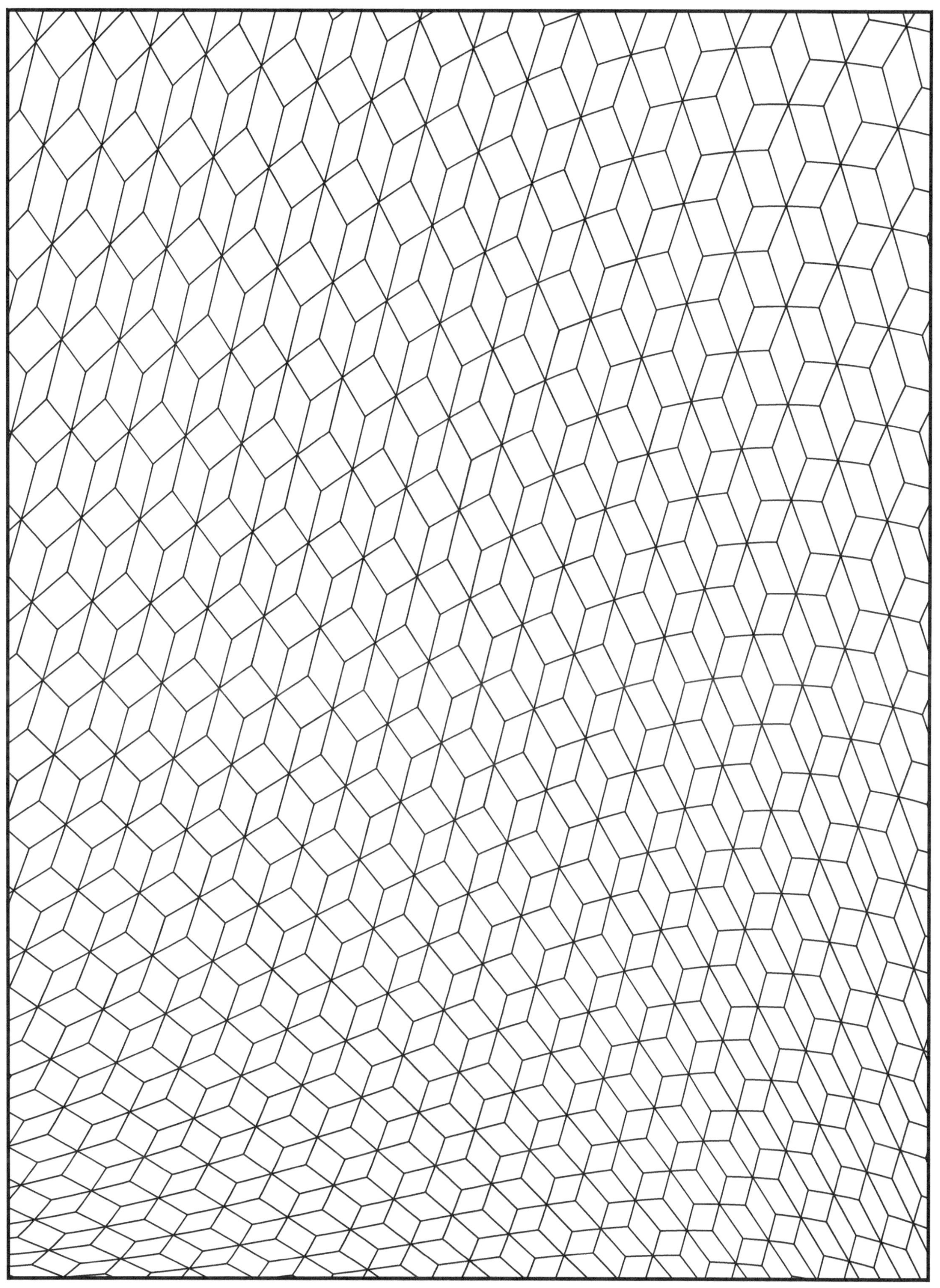

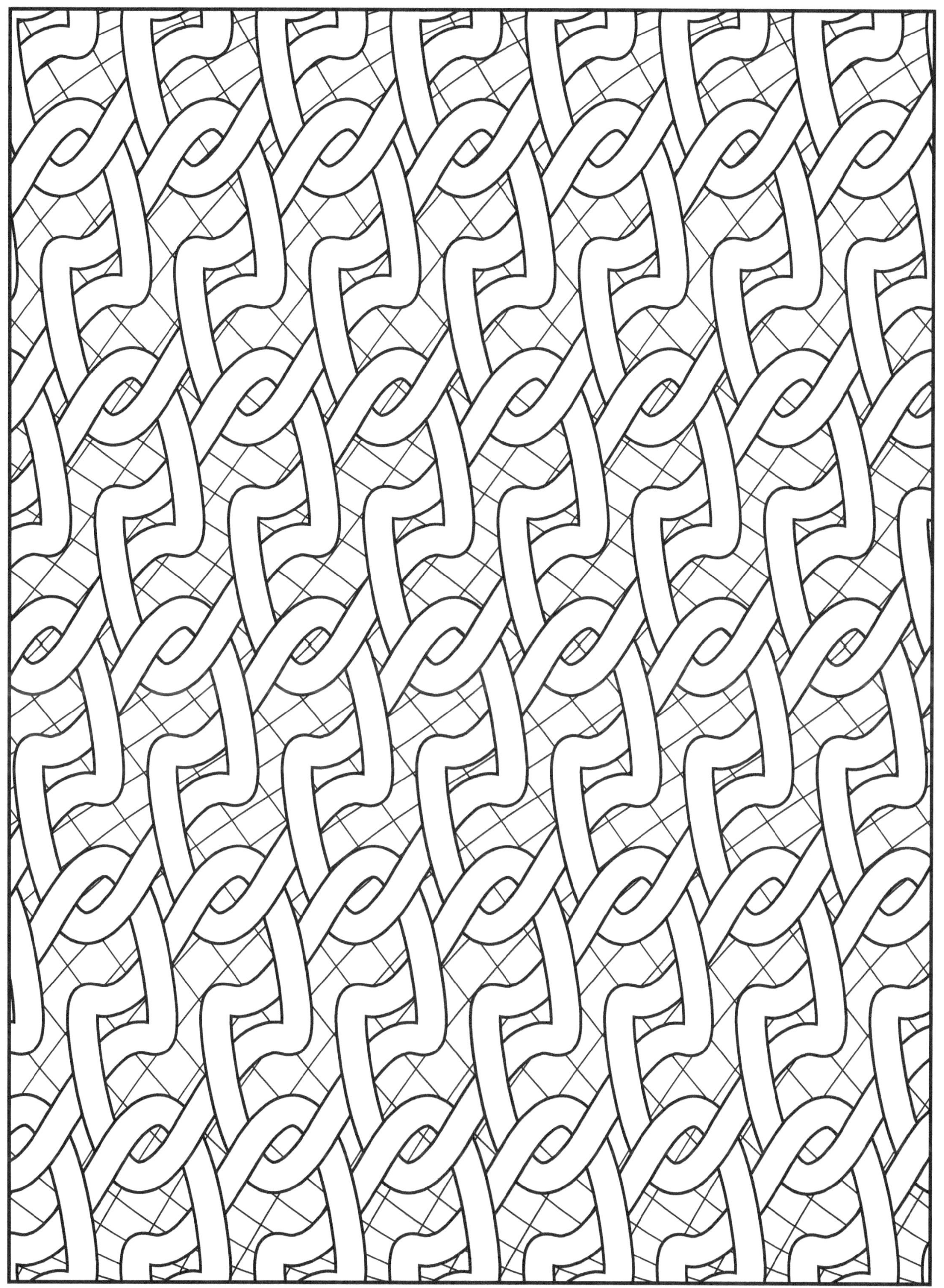

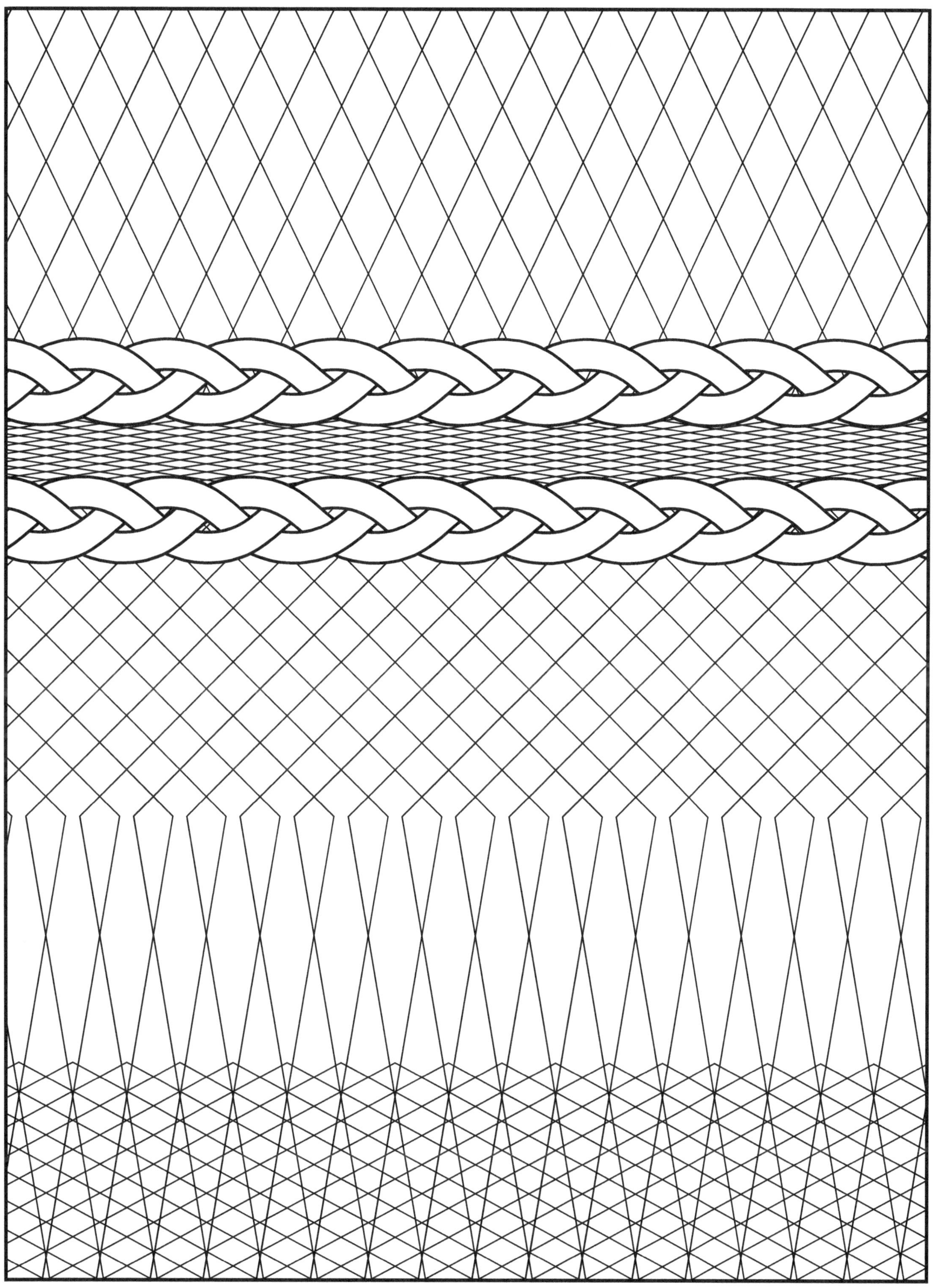

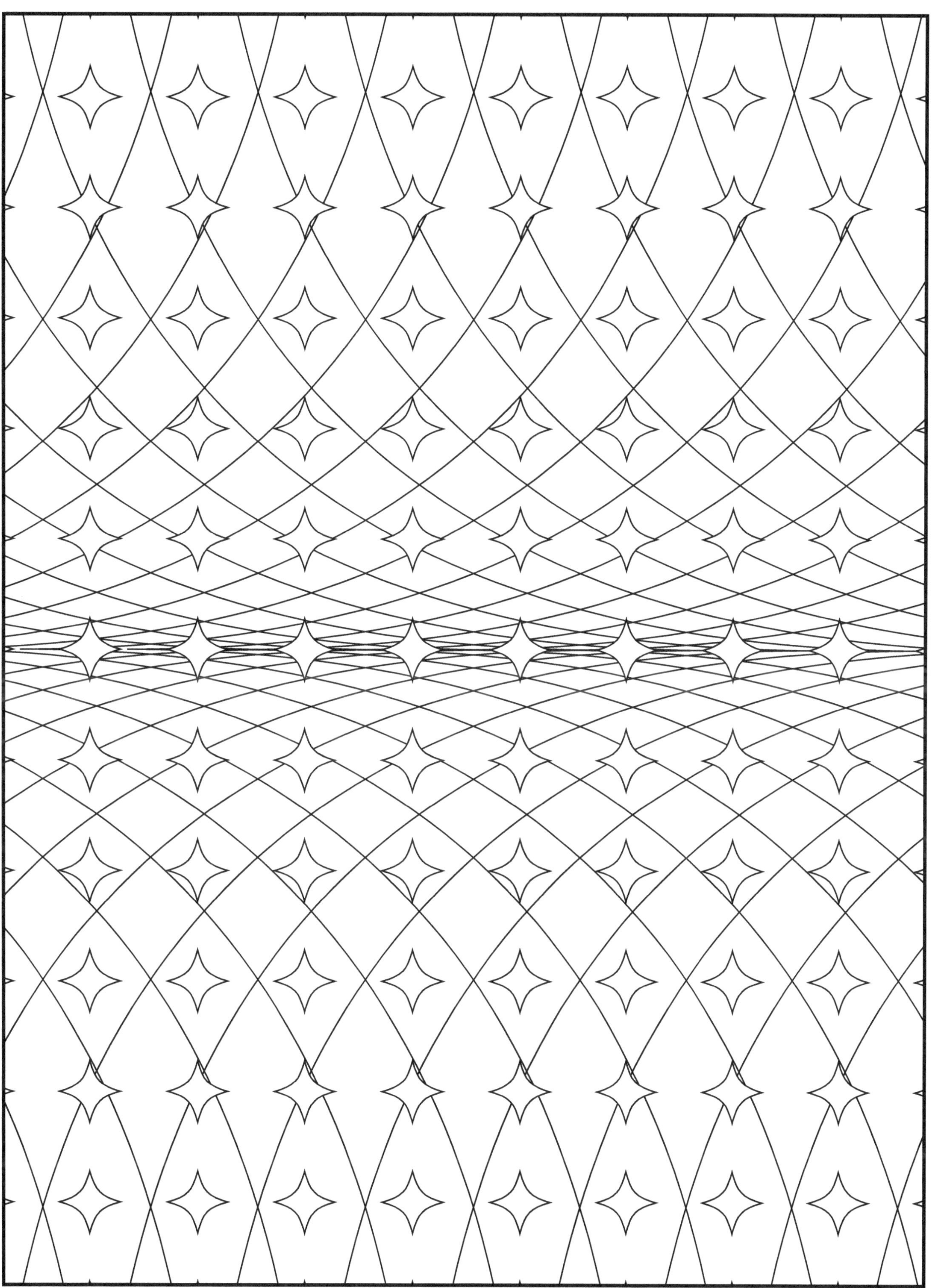

www.ingramcontent.com/pod-product-compliance
Lightning Source LLC
Chambersburg PA
CBHW081732250726
48657CB00010B/3240